MW00440172

MINI-GUIDES

ARMOR IN NORMANDY: THE GERMANS....

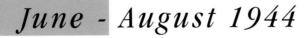

June - August 1944

by Alexandre THERS

Lay-out by the author - Computer drawings by Yann-Erwin ROBERT
Translated from the French by Jonathan NORTH

h&c
PARIS

GERMAN ARMOR IN 1944

After nearly five years of constant fighting, Germany still fielded 32 armored divisions belonging to the Heer (the Army) and the Waffen-SS, as well as numerous independent tank units, but at dawn on June 6, only two of those divisions were in Normandy. The massive scale of the Allied invasion however, drew a reaction and soon a dozen more armor divisions were converging on the beachhead. How strong were these units? What doctrine would they employ against the Allies? How were the divisions structured? What equipment was available to them? And what was their combat ability?

THE PANZER DIVISION IN 1944

German dominance in large-scale armored attacks had brought resounding victory in the early years of the war. During each of those amazing operations, the Panzer divisions had served as the spear-point for each attack. As the war continued the number of Panzer divisions steadily grew: in 1940 there were 10, and by 1942 this had increased to 25.

But lack of personnel and equipment soon began to make themselves felt and this, coupled with the impossibility of competing with the massive industrial capacity of their enemies, made a reorganization of the armored division imperative. So it was that in 1944 the Germans adopted a new structure which now bore little resemblance to the units which had crushed the French in May and June 1940.

Changes in combat techniques, the impact of more effective anti-tank weapons and a massive increase in the power and armor thickness of tanks also influenced the reform. In 1944 the division format was fixed at 14.727 men compared to the 15.600 of 1941 and 1942. Tank regiments (Panzer-regiment), the backbone of the armored division, now consisted of just two battalions of 48 tanks, whereas previously there had been three. Each battalion had four companies. In theory one battalion was to be equipped with the Panzer IV whilst the other was to use the newer Panther.

The tank regiments also benefited from specific support, as each division boasted two regiments of Panzergrenadiers (mechanized infantry), an armored reconnaissance unit and

a tank-destroyer battalion. The divisional artillery consisted of a regiment of mobile artillery and a Flak Group. Other organic units were an engineer battalion, a signals battalion, a depot battalion, divisional trains, a recovery unit, a supply unit and a medical detachment. So, with its theoretical strength of 160 tanks, 28 tank-destroyers, 30 self-propelled guns and 300 half-tracks, the Panzer Division remained a remarkably powerful foe although not quite as formidable as it would have been in 1943.

EQUIPMENT

German AFVs employed in Normandy fall into the following categories:

Assault or Combat Tanks

These were usually armed with a 75 mm or 88 mm gun mounted on a rotating turret. Intended to be as adaptable as possible, they were designed to take on not only enemy armor but also to act against non-armored objectives.

Assault Guns (Sturmgeschütze)

These were a compromise between an assault tank and a self-propelled gun. Initially designed to provide close support to infantry they were also called on to knock out machinegun nests and anti-tank obstacles. Flexible and capable, these machines were easier and cheaper to produce than tanks and they soon took on a prominent role. This role evolved as the infantry were employed more defensively as the war progressed. Indeed, the assault guns were soon used almost exclusively in the role of tank destroyers and they proved their worth through their mobility and their ability to absorb enemy fire.

Tank-Destroyers (Jagdpanzer)

Developed specifically to take on enemy armor, these machines were initially anti-tank guns mounted on the chassis of any obsolete tank, the crew sheltering behind insufficient armor in an open-topped compartment and with no protection to the rear.

These improvised vehicles were created to cope with the massive numbers of tanks encountered on the Eastern Front, most notably the T-34. Such vehicles evolved slowly but were developed into vehicles specifically designed to perform the anti-tank role, given a powerful gun, a sleek, low outline and exceptionally think armor. Unlike the tank, these Jagdpanzers had no turret.

This would prove to be something of a handicap but that was the price to be paid when producing a simple vehicle relatively cheaply. It was Guderian who hastened production of the Jagdpanzer when he realized the significance of the problem besetting German industrial output.

Generally, German armor had significant qualities but also some serious drawbacks. German assault tanks were on the whole, superior to anything the Anglo-Americans had. The Tiger, brought into service in 1942, and the Panther, which appeared in mid-1943, certainly outclassed Allied vehicles. The Panzer IV, initially developed in 1938, was now showing its age, despite frequent modifications, but it still boasted an excellent gun and proved equal to its Allied counterpart, the Sherman medium tank. The fourth most common German armored vehicle in Normandy was the Sturmgeschütz III assault gun, but this again was nearly matched by Allied armor deployed in this theater Again, its true strength lay in its armament: its gun was more powerful than the Sherman's 75 mm but it was equaled by the 76.2 mm gun mounted in some Sherman variants. Generally, German tanks were slower than their American equivalents. But given the fact that the rest of the Heer lacked mobility, German armor was in any case, going to be called upon to act defensively.

THE CONTEXT

Those German armored units which took part in the battles for Normandy fell into two categories: the Heer (or Army) divisions, and those belonging to the Waffen-SS. In theory they were of equal strength, since on paper they consisted of 96 Panther IVs and 76 Panthers. The chief problem for those divisions heading to Normandy was the total domination of the skies by Allied aircraft. In fact, Allied superiority was more of a psychological than a material problem and convoys on the whole suffered insignificant losses. Even so the majority of the bridges over the Seine between Paris and the coast were cut by Allied air raids, something which added to German discomfort.

Some units however made good progress, traveling 250 miles in just two days. The other significant problem for German armored units was the lack of fuel. Allied air power contributed to the scarcity of fuel, but the problem had already been felt in 1942 and in any case, the Eastern Front was to have fuel priority.

The bulk of fuel produced in German-occupied Europe was heading East and the lack of fuel was therefore keenly felt by armored divisions stationed in France. The relatively few depots in Normandy contained little fuel anyway. The one nearest the front line was at Domfront, 50 miles from Caen, and it held 48,000 cubic feet of fuel.

Once the German armored divisions arrived at the front they were quickly scattered in the 'bocage' and began to learn the distinctive features of warfare in such terrain. The typical Norman bocage consisted of tall, thick hedges and sunken, twisted roads, which favored those adept at camouflage and deception. On the other hand, it made life difficult for tanks as the thick hedges prevented progress and impeded visibility and mobility.

In conclusion it should be mentioned that Allied air superiority did not in itself destroy German tanks, but by making German armor remain under cover in daylight hours, and by hitting and destroying convoys carrying supplies and fuel, it forced the Germans to break their armor into small groups, preventing concentrations which might have proved significant, and even prevented certain units from reaching the front.

5

THE PANZER IV

By 1944 the Panzer IV was the oldest German tank still in production but it still continued to form the backbone of the Panzer divisions. For that reason it was the tank most frequently encountered in Normandy.

The Panzer IV was the most common German tank. In 1944 German tank production stood at 19,000 tanks of all kinds. (RR)

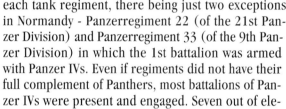

A track link from a Panzer IV. (Collection Van Onsem)

....

Below: A Panzer IV belonging to II. Abteilung of the 12th SS Panzer Regiment, part of the Hitlerjugend division. (Bundesarchiv)

The tank's excellent design dated from before the war but in the course of time the basic concept was modified and adapted so each year it seemed to get more powerful. It was more or less the equal of a Sherman, but despite suffering from poor mechanical reliability, light armor and poor mobility, its 75 mm L/48 gun was far more effective than that mounted on its American rival. Another slight advantage which the Panzer IV possessed was its electrical mechanism for rotating the turret, as it was safer than a hydraulic system which added to the risks of fire should the tank be hit. The most common version of the tank in Normandy was the Ausführung H, brought out in 1943, and the Ausf. J which appeared in March 1944 and differed from the previous version by the removal of the two-stroke motor driving the turret-rotating mechanism in favor of an additional fuel tank. The tank was issued to the 2nd battalion of each tank regiment, there being just two exceptions in Normandy - Panzerregiment 22 (of the 21st Panzer Division) and Panzerregiment 33 (of the 9th Panzer Division) in which the 1st battalion was armed with Panzer IVs. Even if regiments did not have their full complement of Panthers, most battalions of Panzer IVs were present and engaged. Seven out of ele-

A hybrid Panzer IV belonging to the Panzer Lehr Division. Types H and J were the most frequently encountered Panzer IVs in Normandy.
(Illustration by Jean Restayn)

TECHNICAL DATA

(Ausführung H)

Crew: 5.
Weight: 26 tons.
Engine: 12-cylinder Maybach HL 120 TRM gasoline engine, 300 hp.
Max. speed on road: 38 km/h
- across country: 16 km/h
Max. range on road: 210 km
Max. range across country: 130 km
Fuel capacity: 470 liters.
Length (without gun): 7,2 m.
Width with side hull shields: 3,33 m.
Width without side shields: 2,88 m.
Height: 2,68 m.
Armament: 1 X 75-mm KwK 40 L/48 gun, 2 x 7,92-mm MGs
Ammunition: 87 shells, 3.150 MG rounds.
Armor thickness (max.): 80 mm.
Radio: FuG5 set

*L*eft: *An explosive shell casing, as fired by the Panzer IV's 75 mm KwK 40 gun. (Private Collection)*

*O*pposite: *A Panzer IV, Ausf. H or J, belonging to the 12th SS Panzer Division (Hitlerjugend). (Bundesarchiv)*

ven battalions of Panzer IVs consisted of companies boasting 22 tanks. Six out of the eleven went into action with their full complement. In total 897 Panzer IVs were sent to Normandy.

The Panzer V 'Panther'

The Panther was a brilliant combination of firepower, mobility and armor and can probably be considered the best German tank of the war.
It benefited from a robust constitution and despite initial teething troubles, soon boasted an adequate record of reliability, although like most German tanks of the period, the ratio between engine power and tank weight was not ideal.

*T*his Panther has fallen into British hands. Quite a few Panzers with mechanical faults were simply abandoned, and sometimes scuttled by their crews. *(IWM)*

*R*ight: This bag collected spent rounds from the Panther turret machine gun. *(Van Onsem collection)*

*B*elow: Two Panthers meet on a Normandy road. The one on the right is a Befehlpanzer V, Panther Ausf. A, and has the antenna of a command vehicle. It probably belongs to the 9th or 10th SS division. *(Bundesarchiv)*

The Panther's frontal armor surpassed that of most heavy tanks and its superb armament allowed it to fire accurate, high-performance rounds. For a tank of this type it was relatively cheap to produce (a Panther cost 117,000 Marks whilst a Tiger I cost 300,000 Marks). On the other hand, it suffered from transmission and suspension problems. Its running gear gave the tank good weight distribution but made handling difficult.

Most Panzerregiment's 1st battalions were issued with Panthers and that was the case in Normandy apart from Panzerregiment 33, whose 2nd battalion had Panthers, and Panzerregiment 22 which had two battalions of Panzer IVs. Some other units engaged in Normandy (such as Panzerregiment 16 and SS-Panzerregiment 10) were also without Panthers. So it was that out of 10 regiments

TECHNICAL DATA

(Ausführung A)

Crew: 5
Weight: 45.5 tons
Engine: 12-Cyl. Maybach HL 230 P 30 gasoline engine, 700 hp
Max. speed on road: 46 km/h
- across country: 24 km/h
Range on road: 160 km
Fuel capacity: 730 liters
Length with gun: 8.86 m
Length without gun: 6.87 m
Width: 3.27 m
Height: 3.1 m
Armament: 1 x 75 mm KwK 40 L/70 gun, 3 x 7.92 mm machineguns
Ammunition: 79 shells, 5.100 MG rounds
Armor thickness (max.): 100 mm
Radio: FuG5 set

A Panther from the 1st SS-PzDiv 'Leibstandarte SS-Adolf Hitler.' In June 1944 the only SS armored divisions with Panthers were the 9th and 12th SS divisions. (Bundesarchiv)

S S-Oberscharführer Ernst Barkmann 's Panther V Ausf G. Part of the 2nd SS Division ('Das Reich'), Barkmann cleared a path through the American lines on July 27, destroying 14 enemy tanks. (Illustration by Jean Restayn)

deployed in the theater, only 7 had a Panther battalion and many of those were equipped with fewer tanks than the theoretical complement of 17.

A total of 654 Panthers fought in Normandy.

R ight: A Panther episcope. This optical device used mirrors and was fitted as standard to combat tanks. (Van Onsem collection)

The Panzer VI 'Tiger I'

When this tank first appeared in 1942, it was the most powerful in the world. But, by 1944, it was being outclassed by the Panther, the Tiger II and the Soviet Josef Stalin tanks.

Tigers fought as autonomous vehicles, fuel supplies permitting. But their consumption of gasoline was impractically high. Like the Panther, the Tiger's turret was rotated manually. (Private Collection)

....

Right: The 'Tigerfibel' was a comic-style user manual for Tiger crews. (Private Collection)

....

Below: Tiger No 211 belonged to schwere SS-Panzer Abteilung 102. (©ECPAD/France)

The Tiger's side and rear armor was thicker than that of the Panther but its frontal armor was less effective. Its 88-mm gun had less piercing power than the Panther's 75-mm, and in terms of mobility, it was also inferior. In addition it was slow and guzzled gasoline and because of its complexity it was realtively expensive to produce. 105 Tigers had been produced by April 1944. However, it did possess significant advantages. Its shot could penetrate most Anglo-American AFVs, even from a considerable distance, and despite its rectangular shape its armor could deflect the majority of Allied shells, especially if they hit the front of the tank. Only the Sherman Firefly's 17-pounder had a chance and even then, only at medium range.

While most tanks at that time were steered by levers, the Tiger had the advantage of a simple steering wheel. The Tiger's gearbox had eight forward gears and four for reverse, a design which enabled a smooth ride for a such a bulky machine. Theoretically the

D 656/27 Die Tigerfibel ...sooo' ne schnelle Sach

TECHNICAL DATA

Crew: 5
Weight: 57 tons
Engine: 12-cyl. Maybach HL 230 P 45 gasoline engine, 700 hp
Max. speed on road: 38 km/h
- across country: 10-20 km/h
Range on road: 140 km
Fuel capacity: 534 liters
Length with gun: 8.45 m
Width with mudguards: 3.7 m
- without mudguards: 3.4 m
Height: 2.93 m
Armament: 1 x 88 mm KwK 36 I/56 gun, 3 x 7.92 mm MGs
Ammunition: 92 shells, 4,500 MG rounds
Armor thickness (max.): 100 mm
Radio: FuG5

A Tiger of schwere Panzer Abteilung 101. This unit was deployed around Caen in August 1944. The Tiger was relatively immobile and relied upon its defensive capabilities. It was most frequently used to plug breaches and cover tactical withdrawals. (Illustration by Jean Restayn)

Tiger went to equip heavy battalions kept as HQ reserve or assigned to Panzer Corps, and only three Tiger battalions served in Normandy - SS s. Panzer Abteilung 101 and 102 (45 tanks each) and two out of the three companies of s. Panzer-Abteilung 503 (33 tanks).

It also seems that Panzer-Kompanie 316, attached to the Panzer Lehr Division, had three Tigers when it arrived in Normandy, and in all, 126 Tiger Is fought in Normandy.

R ight: A radio receiver Ukw.E.h., part of the FuG5 radio set. This was the kind most commonly used in German armor. (Private Collection)

O pposite: Another view of the 211. Here the tank is fitted with all-metal tracks. These, along with the muzzle brake on the main gun, were modifications which characterized the late Tiger variants. (Bundesarchiv)

THE PANZER VI B 'TIGER II'

Also known as the King Tiger, the Type B Panzer VI was the high point of German World War II heavy tanks. It was a heavier version of the original Tiger, with reinforced and angled armor plating that could withstand most projectiles on the battlefield. It was also equipped with a main gun which surpassed that of the Tiger I.

There was no way that British or American armor could withstand a gun as powerful as the 88 mm Pak 43/3 L/71. It could pierce armor 132 mm thick from a range of 2,000 meters (the Panther could manage 106 mm, the Tiger 82 mm).
(Bovington Tank Museum)

....

Right: A Kwk 43 anti-tank round as fired by the Tiger II.
(Private Collection)

....

Bottom: Tiger IIs on the parade ground of Mailly-le-Camp in July 1944.
(Bovington Tank Museum)

The new 88-mm Pak 43/3L/71 housed in a spacious turret could penetrate 200 mm of armor from a range of 1,000m but was so effective that it could knock out a Sherman or a Cromwell from 3,500m. Its maximum range was 10 km.

However its faults outweighed its advantages: its extra 13 tonnes had not warranted a correspondingly more powerful power unit, as this remained the same as the Panther's.

The King Tiger therefore burned vast amounts of fuel (500 liters to cover 100 km) and consequently, speed, autonomy and mobility were restricted, despite the tank's 80-cm wide combat tracks. These should have helped it master rougher terrain, but because of the additional weight, even that advantage was negated. The tank's transmission and steering were the same as those used in the Tiger I but they were somewhat more delicate and the engine needed constant servicing to keep it running.

Finally, the King Tiger inherited a mediocre gun mount within the tank turret. The weight of the shot

TECHNICAL DATA

Crew: 5
Weight: 68 tons
Engine: 12-cyl. Maybach HL 230 P 30 gasoline engine, 700 hp
Max. speed on road: 38 km/h
- across country: 17 km/h
Range on road: 110-120 km
Range across country: 80 km
Fuel capacity: 860 liters
Length with gun: 10.28 m
Length without gun: 7.26 m
Width with mudguards: 3.75 m
Width without mudguards: 3.65 m
Height: 3.09 m
Armament: 1 x 88 mm KwK 43 L/71 gun, 3 x 7.92 mm MGs
Ammunition: 86 shells, 5.850 MG rounds
Armor thickness (max.): 180 mm
Radio: FuG5 or FuG2 set

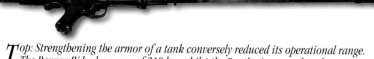

Top: Strengthening the armor of a tank conversely reduced its operational range. The Panzer IV had a range of 210 km whilst the Panther's was reduced to 160 km. That of the Tiger II was limited to some 110-120 km. (Illustration by Jean Restayn)

....

Above: An MG 34 machine gun adapted for use on board tanks. (Private Collection)

(some 20kg) meant that the main gun could not elevate properly. Some 12 Tiger IIs fought in Normandy.

Opposite: The end of a Tiger II belonging to schwere Panzer Abteilung 503. The sleek Porsche turret presented a difficult target for Allied gunners but it was relatively weak at the base. (Bovington Tank Museum)

THE STURMGESCHÜTZE

These assault guns were assigned to three types of units: artillery self-propelled batteries, anti-tank battalions organic to armored divisions and General Reserve assault gun brigades.

A n optic sight used on German armor.
(Van Onsem collection)

O riginally an infantry support AFV, the Stug was more and more used as an anti-tank gun. A variant of the assault gun was therefore developed for the infantry role. The only difference was in its cannon, a 105-mm gun that took the place of the anti-tank gun. This was called the Sturmhaubitze H42 (assault gun H42).
(Bovington Tank Museum)

While not intended to equip Panzer divisions as such, the StuGs could however be called upon to replace tanks unavailable to armored units. For example, the tank battalions attached to Panzergrenadier divisions were composed almost entirely of these vehicles. This was the case with SS-Panzer Abteilung 17 of the 'Götz von Berlichingen' division and the 5th and 6th Abteilungen of the 2nd SS-Panzer Regiment ('Das Reich'), the 7th and 8th Abteilungen of the 9th SS-Panzer Regiment ('Hohenstaufen') and those of the 10th SS-Panzer Regiment (10th SS-Panzer Division, 'Frundsberg'). The most common assault gun was the StuG III, on a Panzer III chassis. The variant most frequently encountered in Normandy was the StuG III, Ausf.G. It was a very reliable vehicle with a low profile and good armament. It was also cheaper to manufacture than an actual tank, as nearly four could be constructed for the price tag of a single Tiger II. As a result, StuGs vastly outnumbered Tigers. Four Stug brigades were deployed in Normandy - Sturmgeschütz-Brigade 341, 394, 902 and Fallschirm-Sturmgeschütz-Brigade 12 (paratroopers). Each had a theoretical strength of 31 vehicles apart from the 341st Brigade which had 45. The first three units were pretty much up to strength when they were sent to the front but evidence is lacking as to the strength of the paratrooper brigade. A few infantry divisions also had StuGs, albeit in an ungenerous manner. Six divisions boasted a 10-Stug company in their Panzerjäger-Abteilung. The 16th Luftwaffe Field Division was also issued with the vehicle, receiving 8 StuG IIIs on July 9. The 1st SS-Panzer Division ('Leibstandarte SS Adolf Hitler') and the 2nd SS Panzer Division ('Das Reich') were also assigned StuGs and assigned them into their Panzerjäger-Abteilung. The 9th and 10th SS Panzer divisions went without

TECHNICAL DATA
(StuG III Ausf. G)
Crew: 4
Weight: 23.9 tons
Engine: 12 cyl. Maybach HL 120 TRM gasoline engine, 300 hp
Max. speed on road: 40 km/h
Range on road: 155 km
- across country: 95 km
Fuel capacity: 310 liters
Length with gun: 8.28 m
Length without gun: 6.85 m
Width: 3.65 m
Height: 2.16 m
Armament: 1 x 75 mm StuK 40L/48 gun, 2 x 7.92 mm MGs
Ammunition: 54 shells, 600 MGrounds
Armor thickness (max.): 80 mm
Radio: FuG15 or FuG16 set

*R*ight: Shoulder strap for an SS non-commissioned officer in a Panzer or anti-tank unit.
(P. Schuber Collection)

*O*pposite: From mid-1943 German StuGs and StuHs began to carry additional armor plating. These armored skirts, or 'Schürzen', were designed to prematurely detonate armor-piercing shells.
(Bovington Tank Museum)

*T*he StuG III was one of three types of assault gun used in Normandy. Apart from the H42, there was also the StuG IV, identical to the StuG III but for its Panzer IV chassis, from which it took its name. The Germans made no distinction between the StuG III and IV, and the IV was only made in very small quantities.
(Illustration by Jean Restayn)

Panzerjäger-Abteilung but two tank companies, which normally would have had Panzer IVs, were equipped with StuG IIIs. The 9th SS Panzer Division had 40 StuGs and the 10th SS Panzer Division boasted 38. The 9th Panzer Division had six StuG IIIs whilst the 116th Panzer Division had only five. The 17th SS-Panzergrenadier Division ('Götz von Berlichingen') had a battalion equipped with 42 StuGs. There were also six StuGs in the Funklenk (radio-control) unit within Panzer-Abteilung 301 and the Funklenk unit of Panzer-Kompanie 316 had 10. Finally the 10 StuG IIIs of the 348th Infantry Division left for the front on July 30. In all some 520 StuGs and Sturmhaubitze (self-propelled infantry gun) were sent to Normandy.

THE STURMPANZER IV 'BRUMMBÄR'

This AFV belonged to a class of vehicles known as assault tanks. It was originally designed to support infantry as they moved forwards. The Brummbär could destroy strongpoints, bunkers and other fortifications.

The first six examples of the Brummbär came into service in 1943. The vehicle was officially designated 'Sturmpanzer IV' in January 1944. The word Brummbär means brown bear and it was nothing more than a nickname. (RR)

Portable inspection lamp as used on German transport and armor. (Private Collection)

Opposite: This photo was taken at Ondefontaine on August 6th 1944. British troops are busy examining a destroyed Brummbär. In all it seems that just 28 Brummbärs were involved in the fighting in Normandy. (IWM B8738)

The Brummbär was fitted with an impressive armament - a 150 mm howitzer which fired a very powerful explosive shell. Unfortunately the weak initial velocity of the shell rendered the gun relatively useless when engaging tanks. Another handicap was the fact that the vehicle could only stow 38 shells, and each weighed 38kgs. Indeed the weight of the gun and armor was such that it was almost too much for the Panzer IV 's chassis. This armor guaranteed the crew a certain amount of protection, but the Brummbär also lacked a machinegun, so it could offer little by way of close-range resistance. Consequently, it relied upon infantry support to protect it from tank-killer teams. The tank's rather delicate suspension and its poor transmission led to many of the vehicles being abandoned. A few were used as command vehicles (Befehlsturmpanzer IV), equipped with radios and adequate antennae. In Normandy, a single unit, the Sturmpanzer-Abteilung 217, was specifically equipped with the vehicle. Between 16 and 28 saw action at the front.

TECHNICAL DATA

Crew: 5
Weight: 28.2 tons
Engine: 12-cyl. Maybach HL 120 TRM gasoline engine, 300 hp
Max. speed on road: 38 km/h
- across country: 15-18 km/h
Range on road: 210 km
- across country: 130 km
Fuel capacity: 470 liters
Length: 5.93 m
Width: 2.88 m
Height: 2.52 m
Armament: 1 x 150-mm StuH 43 L/12 howitzer, up to 2 x 7.92 mm machineguns
Ammunition: 38 shells, 600 MG rounds
Armor thickness (max.): 100 mm
Radio: FuG5 or FuG2 set

*T*here were a good number of teething problems with the Brummbär. For one, it was too heavy for its engine. The only problem which the Germans failed to overcome was the engine's poor fuel capacity. The howitzer could be elevated from - 8 to 30 degrees and rotated 15 degrees to the left and the right.
(Illustration by Jean Restayn)

*O*pposite: A power unit as used in German radio receivers Ukw.E.e and Ukw.E.b. (with the FuG5 tank set). This was one of two kinds of power units used in German armor.
(Van Onsem Collection)

*O*pposite: A good view of the rear of a Brummbär. Its hull is covered in 'Zimmerit' anti-magnetic paste.
(RR)

This Marder III was destroyed by American artillery.
(National Archives)

A black leather holster for the P38 pistol. Along with the P08 Luger this handgun was most common in the German armed forces and therefore a prized souvenir for Allied soldiers.
(Militaria Magazine)

THE 'MARDER III'

The SdKfz 138 Marder (Marten) tank destroyer was something of a transition between the first rudimentary self-propelled guns and the sophisticated assault guns which later appeared.

The Marder was based on the excellent Czech LT 38 chassis which was extremely reliable as well as being simple and sleek. Variant M was the final version to take the field. The vehicle was perhaps a little top heavy but it was significantly better than its predecessors in terms of armor.

Earlier models in fact had such weak armor that it didn't even protect the crew from small arms fire. The engine was positioned in the center of the vehicle, which improved balance and accuracy of fire.

The machine gun was removed from the hull and placed next to the cannon. This cheap vehicle proved itself remarkably effective in anti-tank warfare. The Marder could be found in use by most infantry divisions' tank destroyer battalions (Panzerjäger-Abteilung) in Normandy.

The theoretical scale of issue was 14 vehicles but in reality only a few companies received their full complement. Panzer divisions were not officially issued with Marders at this point in the war but it seems that the 9th Panzer Division had nine. The vehicle was to be phased out in favor of the Jagdpanzer IV but none of these vehicles arrived in Normandy.

TECHNICAL DATA

(Ausführung M)

Crew: 4
Weight: 10.5 tons
Engine: Praga AC, gasoline, 150 hp
Max. speed on road: 42 km/h
Range on road: 190 km
Fuel capacity: 218 liters
Length with gun: 4.95 m
Width: 2.15 m
Height: 2.48 m
Armament: 1 x 75-mm PaK 40/3 L/46 gun, 1 x 7.92 mm MG
Ammunition: 27 shells, 600 MG rounds
Armor thickness (max.): 20 mm
Radio: FuG Spr d set

*P*revious page: a factory-fresh Marder III Ausf. M. Panzer divisions were not supposed to be issued with Marders. Even so the 9th Panzer Division had nine and the 17th SS-Panzergrenadier Division 'Götz von Berlichingen' had twelve. (Bundesarchiv)

*T*he Marder III's 75-mm gun could perforate 116 mm of armor with an armor-piercing shell from a distance of 1,000m. *(Illustration by Jean Restayn)*

*B*elow: This photo is of the same vehicle seen on the previous page. The armor on the turret around the gun was so weak that it offered only minimal protection to the crew. As with most tank-destroyers, the Marder's gun was difficult to traverse, managing only between -5 and 13 degrees. *(Bundesarchiv)*

*A*n artillery officer's sidecap, with red arm-of-service piping. *(Militaria Magazine)*

THE JAGDPANZER IV

The Marder, handicapped by its height and its light armor, was not really suited to actual counter-attacks against enemy armor. Most were forced to fire from prepared concealed positions, but this wasn't the case with the Jagdpanzer IV which was much better protected.

An artillery officer's cap. The cockade and eagle are for Heer (army) troops, red is the artillery color. (L. Charbonneau Collection)

A leather identity disk wallet. The greyhound was the 116th Panzer Division formation sign. (Van Onsem collection)

Below: A Jagdpanzer IV belonging to the 116th Panzer Division. (Bundesarchiv)

The Jagdpanzer was specifically designed to take on and defeat enemy armor and it was by and large, successful. It was a simple concept and was built out of parts which already existed and were used in other vehicles (Panzer IV hulls and StuGs). It was quick and easy to build and it was much cheaper than a tank. It had a compact superstructure and frontal armor which was incredibly effective, much more so than that of the Tiger I. The vehicle was also well protected on its sides and it had a lower silhouette than the StuG.

From May 1944 the frontal armor was further reinforced, making it almost as thick as the Panther's. As with the StuG, StuH and Jagdpanther, the vehicle's main gun was difficult to aim and this meant that the crew had to maneuver the vehicle in order to line it up against its intended target. Despite this apparent drawback it was a deadly weapon. The Jagdpanzer IV was designed to equip the Panzerjäger-Abteilungen organic to Panzer divisions. Most of these were then outfitted with StuG IIIs. The 9th and 10th SS-Panzer divisions went without Panzerjäger-Abteilungen in Normandy but were supposed to receive Jagdpanzers in August. The 21st Panzer-Division never received the Jagdpanzer. In June the only two units fitted out with this vehicle were the Panzer-Lehr Division and the 2nd Panzer Division (31 and 21 Jagdpanzers respectively). The Panzerjäger-Abteilung of the 'Hitlerjugend' division was in

TECHNICAL DATA

Crew: 4
Weight: 24 tons
Engine: 12-cyl. Maybach HL 120 TRM gasoline engine, 300 hp
Max. speed on road: 40 km/h
Range on road: 210 km
Range across country: 130 km
Fuel capacity: 470 liters
Length: 6.85 m
Width: 3.17 m
Height: 1.85 m
Armament: 1 x 75-mm PaK 39 L/48 gun,
1 x 7.92 mm machinegun
Ammunition: 55 shells,
600 MG rounds
Armor thickness (max. - except gun mantlet): 60 mm
Radio: FuG Spr f. set

The Jagdpanzer IV was an excellent machine but still had its drawbacks. Chief among these was a tendency for the gun's recoil to disrupt the aiming mechanism. A special system to disperse gun smoke from the crew's compartment was adopted after the Jagdpanzer entered production.
(Illustration by Jean Restayn)

its activation process when the Allied landings took place and it seems that one of its companies had 10 Jagdpanzer in Normandy. On July 10, 21 Jagdpanzers were assigned to the 116th Panzer-Division and 21 were sent to the 9th Panzer-Division on July 20, but these did not fight in Normandy. Finally, 31 vehicles were assigned to the 17th SS-Panzergrenadier Division ('Götz von Berlichingen') around June 30 and saw action around Laval in August. In all some 114 Jagdpanzer IVs were sent to Normandy.

Right: a Jagdpanzer IV belonging to the 116th Panzer Division. The long 75 mm gun tube disturbed the hull balance and wore down the forward wheels and tracks.
In order to solve this problem the two foremost wheels were replaced with wheels made entirely of metal.
(Bundesarchiv)

THE JAGDPANTHER

The Jagdpanther was a superb tank-destroyer. Based in part on the chassis of the Panther, it was fast, sleek and well-proportioned. Armed with the fearsome Pak 43/3 L/71 88-mm cannon (as used on the Tiger II) it was one of the most successful German armored vehicles of the war.

*H*eadphones as issued to Panzer troops (Kopffernhörer).
(Militaria Magazine)

*A*German tank's machine gun transit case.
(Van Onsem collection)

....

*B*elow: These two Jagdpanthers have made it out of the Falaise pocket. Jagdpanther crews benefited from an excellent intercom system.
(Bundesarchiv)

The hull of this new tank-destroyer (it only began to appear in service in early 1944) offered the crew more space than the Panther fighting compartment. Its sloping front and sides were designed to deflect shells and rendered most Allied anti-tank guns ineffective.

The only way of halting this monster was to shoot at its tracks. However the vehicle was hampered by not being able to rotate its gun (there was no turret as such) and it could only rotate 22 degrees and elevate between -8 and 14 degrees. This made for a tank inferior to the Panther in that respect.

But such drawbacks were more than compensated for by its overall efficiency. Its excellent armament fired a special shot, the Panzergranate 40/43, which proved the scourge of all Allied armor. In addition, its gun, mobile, well-balanced and well-designed, performed excellently. Examples built after May 1944 had their gun tubes manufactured in two parts to make replacement easier when the rifling was worn.

The Jagdpanthers equipped heavy tank destroyer battalions

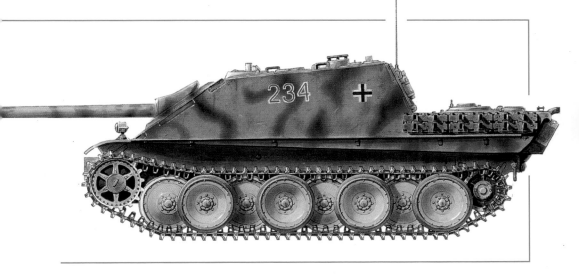

TECHNICAL DATA

Crew: 5
Weight: 45.5 tons
Engine: 12-cyl. Maybach HL 230 P30 gasoline engine, 700 hp
Max. speed on road: 55 km/h
Max. speed across country: 30 km/h
Range on road: 160 km
Range across country: 100 km
Fuel capacity: 720 liters
Length with gun: 9,87 m
Length without gun: 6.60 m
Width with mudguards: 3.42 m
- without mudguards: 3.27 m
Height: 2.72 m
Armament: 1 x 88 mm PaK 43 L/71 gun, 1 x 7.92 mm MG.
Ammunition: 57 shells, 600 MG rounds
Armor thickness (max. - except gun mantle): 80 mm
Radio: FuG5 and FuG2 sets

(schwere Panzerjäger-Abteilung). Each was supposed to be supplied with 45 vehicles. Only one unit however utilized these vehicles in Normandy - the Panzerjäger-Abteilung 654 which arrived quite late at the Norman front.

*A*bove: *This Jagdpanther belongs to the schwere Panzerjäger-Abteilung 654 and is distinguished by its 'Zimmerit' finish. Zimmerit was supposed to prevent magnetic mines sticking to the tank and made its appearance in September 1943. It was phased out in September 1944.*
(Illustration by Jean Restayn)

*B*ottom left: *Accessories for use with the Jagdpanther's machine gun. The butt and the bipod allowed the gun to be used in a ground role.*
(Van Onsem collection)

THE PANZERHAUBITZE 'WESPE'

The Panzerhaubitze (self-propelled howitzer) 105-mm Wespe (wasp) was a vehicle which combined the le. FH18 howitzer, the standard gun of the divisional artillery, with the chassis of a Panzer II.

*T*he frontal armor of the Wespe was weak; it was only 30-mm thick for the hull, 20-mm thick for the superstructure and 10-mm thick for the gun shield. *(RR)*

*R*ight: A 'jerrycan' belonging to an SS unit. It bears the inscription 'fuel, 20 liters, flammable'.
(Van Onsem collection)

*B*elow: A Wespe belonging to the 9th SS-Panzer Division ('Hohenstaufen') in the winter of 1943 to 1944. *(Bundesarchiv)*

The Wespe was brought out in something of a hurry in 1942 to satisfy the demand for a self-propelled howitzer. The vehicle's armor was thin, no more than 10 mm, and provided insufficient protection for the crew.

The vehicle was also limited to 32-round stowage, but it was still an excellent gun and it met with great success. If need be it could also serve as a tank-destroyer.

It served, on the whole, with the Panzerartillerie and was built in great numbers. It outfitted batteries of artillery attached to Panzer divisions and Panzergrenadier divisions.

All armored units in Normandy made use of the vehicle with the exception of the 17th SS-Panzer Division, the 21st Panzer-Division, and the Panzer Lehr Division.

AMIENS 60
ROUEN 78
ABBEVILLE 86
Le TRÉPORT 97

*T*he Wespe was far more reliable than its 'big brother' the Hummel.
(Illustration by Jean Restayn)

*O*pposite: This German map was found in the Falaise pocket. It probably belonged
to a member of the 9th SS-Panzer Regiment (9th SS PzDiv. Hohenstaufen),
or of the schwere SS Panzer Abteilung 102. *(Private Collection)*

*B*elow: The Wespe's elevation was between -5 and 42 degrees.
(DR)

TECHNICAL DATA

Crew: 5
Weight: 11 tons
Engine: Maybach H 62 TR
gasoline engine, 140 hp
Max. speed on road: 40 km/h
- across country: 20 km/h
Range on road: 140 km
Range across country: 95 km
Fuel capacity: 170 liters
Length without gun: 4.81 m
Width: 2.28 m
Height: 2.30 m
Armament: 1 x 105-mm le.
FH18M L/28 howitzer,
1 x 7.92 mm MG
Ammunition: 32 shells,
600 MG rounds
Armor thickness (max.):
30 mm
Radio: FuG Spr f set

THE PANZERHAUBITZE 'HUMMEL'

As with the Wespe, the Hummel (bumblebee) was a hybrid combining a howitzer (in this case a 150-mm) with a tank chassis, in this case the Panzer III or an extended Panzer III chassis. This vehicle filled the gap until a specifically-designed self-propelled gun could be put into production.

*T*his laryngophone *(Keblkopfmikrofon) was used onboard German tanks to reduce ambient noise in radio or intercom transmission. (Militaria Magazine)*

....

*B*elow: Photographs *of Hummels in Normandy are comparatively rare. Here we see examples of the vehicle in France in the winter of 1943 to 1944. They belong to the 9th SS-Panzer Division 'Hohenstaufen.' The two vehicles at the back have had their guns removed so they can act as munitions carriers. (Bundesarchiv)*

Economy was one of the motivating factors behind the creation of the Hummel. It used components which were already widely available or which could easily be adapted, as was the case with the large-caliber gun. The vehicle's superstructure, crew compartment and armament were entirely new concepts when the Hummel came into service in 1942.

The crew compartment was open-topped, which helped the crew to serve the gun. The s. FH18 howitzer could elevate from 30 degrees right up to 42 degrees and could fire a shell 9.5 km (13.2 km if it fired the No 8 explosive charge but this was rarely used). Few shells could actually be stowed onboard but ammunition was carried in Hummels specifically adapted to serve as carriers.

Their guns were removed and the resulting gap in their frontal armor covered over. The Hummel was an excellent armored vehicle. It equipped the heavy artillery batteries of some self-propelled

TECHNICAL DATA

Crew: 6
Weight: 24 tons
Engine: Maybach HL 120 TRM gasoline engine, 300 hp
Max. speed on road: 42 km/h
- across country: 24 km/h
Range on road: 215 km
- across country: 130 km
Fuel capacity: 470 liters
Length without gun: 7.17 m
Width: 2.97 m
Height: 2.81 m
Armament: 1 x 150 mm s. FH18/1, L/30 howitzer, 1 x 7.92 mm MG
Ammunition: 18 shells, 600 MG rounds
Armor thickness (max.): 30 mm
Radio: FuG Spr f

artillery units attached to Panzer divisions. Originally, each armored division had six Hummels in a single heavy battery but later more Panzer divisions fielded a second battery. Some 289 Hummels were produced in 1944.

_A_ shoulder board for a Panzer unit lieutenant. The monogram L for 'Lehr' indicates he belonged to a training school.
(Private Collection)

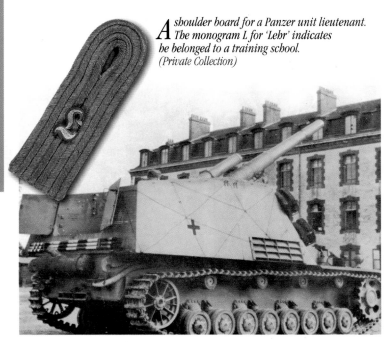

_O_pposite: This photograph shows the massive shape of the Hummel's 150-mm howitzer. The crew's compartment was spacious enough to afford the gunners relative ease of movement.
_(RR)_

THE SdKfz 250/251 ARMORED PERSONNEL CARRIERS

These multi-purpose vehicle were mainly used as a front-line personnel carriers in the Panzerdivisions.

A combat badge awarded to armored infantry (Panzergrenadiers) and armored car crews.
(Militaria Magazine)

B elow: An SdKfz 251/9 Ausf. D, armed with a 75-mm gun for infantry support. During the rare German counter attacks in Normandy, the Panzergrenadiere in such vehicles made better progress than their accompanying tanks.
(Bundesarchiv)

Essentially a superstructure imposed on an artillery tractor's chassis, the SdKfz was an exceptionally good-looking vehicle with its sleek lines and its double doors to the rear (which allowed a quick exit from the vehicle). However its frontal armor was only 14.5 mm thick, that to the rear only 8 mm which meant that the troops inside were really only protected from small arms fire. The high quality of the vehicle, combined with the development of mobile forms of warfare, caused a meteoric rise in the use of the half-track. It was used as a mortar-carrier, liaison vehicle, ammunition carrier, artillery observation post, ambulance, self-propelled 75-mm gun and AA vehicle.

Despite the evident qualities of the vehicle its weaknesses, particularly in terms of armor, became more and more apparent as the conflict dragged on. German units also used captured French Unic and Somua-Kégresse half-tracks. But in 1944 the lighter Sd. Kfz 250 was the main armored personnel carrier in reconnaissance units. The heavier m. SPW (SdKfz 251) was used by engineer battalions as well as one of the two Panzergrenadier-regiments organic to the Panzerdivision. Tank regiments had 10 such APCs and Tiger tank heavy battalions were issued with 11 SdKfz 251.

TECHNICAL DATA

(SdKfz 251 Ausf. D)
Crew: 2
Transport capacity:
10 grenadiers
Weight: 8 tons
Engine: 6-cyl. Maybach HL
42 TUKRM gasoline engine,
100 hp
Max. speed on road: 53 km/h
Range across country:
130 km
Length: 5.98 m
Width: 2.1 m
Height: 1.75 m
Armament: 1 or 2 7.92 mm
machineguns
Ammunition: 600 MG rounds
Armor thickness (max.):
15 mm
Radio: FuG Spr Ger f. set

*T his SPW 250/8 could belong either to the 1st SS-Panzer Division
or to the 2nd. It was armed with redundant short-barreled versions
of the 75-mm tank gun mounted on early Panzer III and IV.
(Illustration by Jean Restayn)*

*B elow: this SdKfz 251/9 used as an ambulance has fallen into British hands.
(IWM)*

*B ottom left: an SdKfz 251 road wheel. Panzer divisions usually included four battalions
of infantry. The fourth battalion was usually transported in half-tracks. SS divisions had
six battalions of infantry, again one was transported by SdKfz 251.
(Van Onsem collection)*

THE FLAKPANZER 38 (t)

This vehicle was the first attempt to equip armored units with mobile Flak support - Flak guns mounted on an armored chassis. Used for the first time in June 1944 it was soon apparent that it was an ineffective weapon, and its single 20-mm gun was incapable of repelling fighter-bombers.

A rear view of one of the early Flakpanzer 38s. (Bundesarchiv)

Z eiss 10 x 50 binoculars as issued to armored units. (Militaria Magazine)

The gun platform was sealed by eight armored shields which provided those inside with insufficient protection. In addition, these shields had to be lowered if the gun was to operate properly, which made the crew particularly vulnerable during air raids. Its chief advantage lay with its Czech LT 38 chassis, a robust and reliable motor. In all 84 Flakpanzer 38 (t) s were used in Normandy.

There were other similar vehicles, such as the 'Möbelwagen' (removal van). Just as with the Flakpanzer, this Flak vehicle had good and bad sides. Its crews complained about the poor armor and the difficulties in operating the 37-mm gun against low-flying fighter-bombers.

From June 15, the 9th, 11th and 116th Panzer-Divisions were equipped with these vehicles. As the military situation deteriorated, the Panzer divisions were reorganized in August and the Möbelwagens were supplemented by four Flakpanzer 38 (t) acting as a command tanks.

TECHNICAL DATA

Crew: 4
Weight: 9.8 tons
Engine: Praga AC gasoline
engine, 140 hp
Max. speed on road: 42 km/h
Range on road: 210 km
Length without gun: 4.61 m
Width: 2.15 m
Height: 2.25 m
Armament: 1 x 20-mm
Flak 38 L/112.5 gun
Ammunition: 1,040 rounds
Armor thickness (max.):
15 mm
Radio: FuG5 or FuG2 set

This Flakpanzer 38 (t) belongs to a Heer unit engaged in Normandy in June 1944. (Illustration by Jean Restayn)

A newly-organized Panzer Brigade was supposed to have four Möbelwagens and the Panzergrenadier divisions had three. A few examples of the Wirbelwind (Tornado), a much more effective vehicle with four 20-mm cannon and 3,200 rounds in a protective turret, fought successfully in Normandy.

Combat badge for Army anti-aircraft gunners. (Militaria Magazine)

Opposite: A good view of the gun platform and its hinged side shields. (Bundesarchiv)

Previous page: Of the 84 Flakpanzer 38 (t) s committed in Normandy, all were either captured or destroyed. (Bundesarchiv)

THE 105-mm HOWITZER
ON A H-39 CHASSIS

One of the consequences of the French defeat in June 1940 was that an enormous number of armored vehicles fell into German hands. The victors modified a number of these, including the Lorraine chassis and the Hotchkiss H-39 tank and these provided a sound base for a number of self-propelled guns.

A self-propelled 105-mm howitzer on a French Hotchkiss tank chassis. With its towering silhouette, it could only perform in a defensive role. (Bovington Tank Museum)

G erman steel helmet, early pattern (1935)
(Private Collection)

A number of vehicles were produced by 'Kompanie Becker' based in Paris. Of the 120 H-39 tank chassis delivered to these workshops, some 60 were converted into tank-destroyers equipped with the 75-mm PaK 40 gun and into 24 self-propelled 105-mm howitzers. The only unit to receive a substantial number of such vehicles was the 21st Panzer Division - its 155th Mechanized Artillery Regiment had 36 vehicles based on the H-39. The tank-destroyers built on the H-39 were renamed 38 H (f) by the Germans.

There were two models; first, the 'Panzerjäger Selbsfahrlafette 7.5 cm PaK 40,' which was comparatively rare, lightly armored and had no hull machine gun. It was a particularly vulnerable vehicle unsuited to close-quarter fighting even against infantry. The 48 such AFVs committed in Normandy were lost.

The '105-mm le. FH 18/40 auf Geschützwagen 38 H (f),' was a self-propelled gun mounted on the H-39 chassis. Some 48 were built and 36 were assigned to the 155th Mechanized Artillery Regiment and 12 to Sturmgeschütz- Abteilung 200. Other variants involving the H-39 chas-

TECHNICAL DATA

Crew: 5
Weight: 12.5 tons
Engine: 6-cyl. Hotchkiss 120 PS gasoline engine, 120 hp
Max. speed on road: 25 km/h
Range on road: 150 km
Length: 5.77 m
Width: 2.55 m
Height: 2.24 m
Armament: 1 x 105-mm howitzer le. FH 18/40, 1 x 7.92 mm MG
Ammunition: 24 shells
Armor thickness (max.): 34 mm
Radio: FuG Spr d. set

*P*revious page: The French H-39 chassis could barely withstand the weight of the howitzer and the gun compartment.
(Bovington Tank Museum)

*P*ushing through the undergrowth the massive outline of this self-propelled howitzer emerges. The gun tube could be elevated between -5 and 22 degrees.
(Bovington Tank Museum)

*T*he self-propelled 105-mm howitzers were heavily involved in Operation Goodwood, and contributed to stop the tank attacks of the 11th Armoured Division. (Illustration by Jean Restayn)

sis were also produced. Some were used as observation posts, with a modified turret, armament and chassis. Some even had their entire superstructure reworked to house a mortar or carry ammunition.

Other ex-French vehicles were delivered to the 21st Panzer-Division. There was the 105-mm self-propelled howitzer on the Lorraine chassis, the Marder I (a designation given to all French vehicles mounting the PaK 40 anti-tank gun), the Somua S35 tank and a great number of Renault UE light tracked carriers transformed into personnel carriers or rocket launchers.

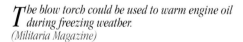

*T*he blow torch could be used to warm engine oil during freezing weather.
(Militaria Magazine)

PRACTICAL INFORMATION

This information focuses on places which saw armored combat or where substantial numbers of tanks played a part in the battle for Normandy. Military-vehicle enthusiasts should note that we list places where actual vehicles can be seen as well bigger museums and commemorative monuments.

CALVADOS

At Port-en-Bessin there is a **unique museum** of underwater artefacts. It is unique in that it presents items dredged up from the sea-bed: tanks, trucks and other vehicles. It's a novel way of rendering homage to the liberators.

Musée des épaves sous-marines du débarquement
Route de Bayeux – BP Commes
14520 Port-en-Bessin
Tel: 02 31 21 17 06

Open everyday from June to 30 September. Open weekends in May, 10.00 to 12.00 and 14.00 to 18.00.

Also worth a visit: three plaques and two steles

Some five miles to the south is Bayeux with its **Battle of Normandy Memorial Museum**. It evokes the 77 days of the campaign, has three galleries and covers a large area. Around a hundred uniforms are on display as well as a **Sherman tank**, an **M10 Tank Destroyer**, a **Churchill** and a **Hetzer** (an interesting vehicle which, however, was not deployed in Normandy). There's also a cinema (150 seat-cinema) showing short films on the campaign.

Musée-Mémorial de la Bataille de Normandie
Boulevard Fabian Ware - BP 21215
14402 Bayeux CEDEX
Tél.: 02 31 92 93 41 - fax: 02 31 21 85 11
www.mairie-bayeux.fr.

Open all year. From 17 September to 30 April, 10.00 to 12.30 and 14.00 to 18.00. From 1 May to 16 September, 09.30 to 18.30. Closed in the second half of January.

Also worth a visit: general de Gaulle's Museum, British Cemetery, monuments, steles and plaques.

From Bayeux head west to Saint-Laurent-sur-Mer. There, not far from Omaha Beach, and close by the American cemetery at Colleville, is the **Omaha Beach Memorial Museum**. Apart from countless artefacts, uniforms and weapons from D-day there are also important records relating to the Resistance and Deportation and details of the economic plight of the region under the Germans. An excellent panorama recreates the landings whilst a **Sherman** and a **155 mm Long Tom** can be seen in the car park as well as a **landing craft**.

Musée d'Omaha Beach à Saint-Laurent-sur-Mer
« Les moulins » - rue de la mer
14710 Saint-Laurent-sur-Mer
Tél.: 02 31 21 97 44 - fax: 02 31 92 72 80
http://www.museememorial-omaha.com

Open from 15 February to 15 March (10.00 to 12.30 and 14.30 to 18.00), 16 March to 15 May (9.30 to 18.30), 16 May to 15 September (09.30 to 19.00 except July-August: 9.30 to 19.30) and from 15 September to 15 November (9.30 to 18.30).

The American cemetery at Saint Laurent/Colleville might also be of interest with its commemorative plaques and monuments.

From Bayeux you can also head east. Five miles to the north-east is the **Arromanches Museum**, built by the site of the Mulberry harbour. There's a **half-track**, a **Sherman** and **two artillery guns**. The diorama, models, films and exhibits cover the whole of Overlord.

Musée du débarquement d'Arromanches
Place du 6 juin
14117 Arromanches
Tél.: 02 31 22 34 31 - fax: 02 31 92 68 83
www.normandy1944.com

Open all year round (except January): from 10.00 to 12.30 and 13.30 to 17.00. In summer opening hours are 09.00 to 19.00.

The **360° museum at Arromanches** is also of interest.

Five miles to the east of Arromanches in the centre of Ver-sur-Mer, by the D 514, is a **British Sexton**. The museum of the **America-Gold Beach** is also here. There are two buildings and exhibits describe the landings as well as the role of the 50th Division in King sector, Gold Beach.

Musée America-Gold Beach
2, place Amiral Byrd
14114 Ver-sur-Mer
Tél. fax: 02 31 22 58 58

Opening hours:
From 10.30 to 13.30 and 14.30 to 17.30 in July and August.
Wednesdays and Thursdays (09.30 to 12.00) from 1 November to 30 April. Closed Tuesdays in May, June, September and October.

Also worth a visit: two monuments, two plaques and a board.

Again to the east is Courseulles-sur-Mer with its **monument to the Royal Winnipeg Rifles** and, close to the sea front, a **Sherman tank** restored in 1970. There are also a number of plaques and monuments in the town. In the adjoining town of Graye-sur-Mer there is a **British Churchill mortar** tank near the Liberation monument.

Six miles from Courseulles, at Lion-sur-Mer, there is a **Churchill AVRE** at the western exit of the town on the D 514. In the neighboring town of Hermanville-sur-Mer, and again by the D 514, there is a **British Centaur** and the **British cemetery** with its 1,005 graves and four monuments.

Not far from the beach at Ouistreham, is the **Atlantic Wall Museum**. This is located in a vast bunker, the former HQ commanding all the batteries along the Orne estuary. It gives the visitor a real insight into the way such defences functioned. The rooms are on five levels and have been fitted out just as they were. There are boiler rooms, sleeping quarters, a pharmacy, a hospital, magazines, communication rooms and an observation post fitted with a powerful range-finder.

Musée du bunker du Mur de l'Atlantique
Boulevard du 6 juin
14150 Ouistreham-Riva-Bella
Tél.: 02 31 97 28 69 - fax: 02 31 96 66 05
e. mail: bunkermusee@aol.com

Opening hours:
10.00 to 18.00 from 3 February to 15 November
09.00 to 19.00 from 1 April to 30 September
Closed 16 November to 2 February